Silent City

By

Sophia Pagan

Silent City is an experiment in slowing down urban culture by taking just one second out of time. The goal is to consciously step out of the rush of city life and discover the silence amid the chaos. Within this one second is where Sophia believes, "We stop thinking and start feeling. It's where we find the moments that reconnect us to ourselves, to each other and to the world." Silent City is a stunning collection of images taken out of time, daring viewers to do the same.

Silent City tente une analyse sur les effets de lenteur de la culture urbaine sur les gens en s'arrêtant juste une seconde hors du temps. L'objectif est de sortir consciemment du tumulte de la ville et de découvrir le silence au sein du chaos. En l'espace de cette seconde, nous nous trouvons dans ce que Sophia considère être l'instant où «nous cessons de penser et où nous commençons à ressentir. C'est là que nous trouvons les moments pour nous reconnecter à nous-mêmes, aux uns, aux autres et au monde.» Silent City est une étonnante collection d'images prises hors du temps, incitant les spectateurs d'en faire de même.

www.SophiaPagan.com

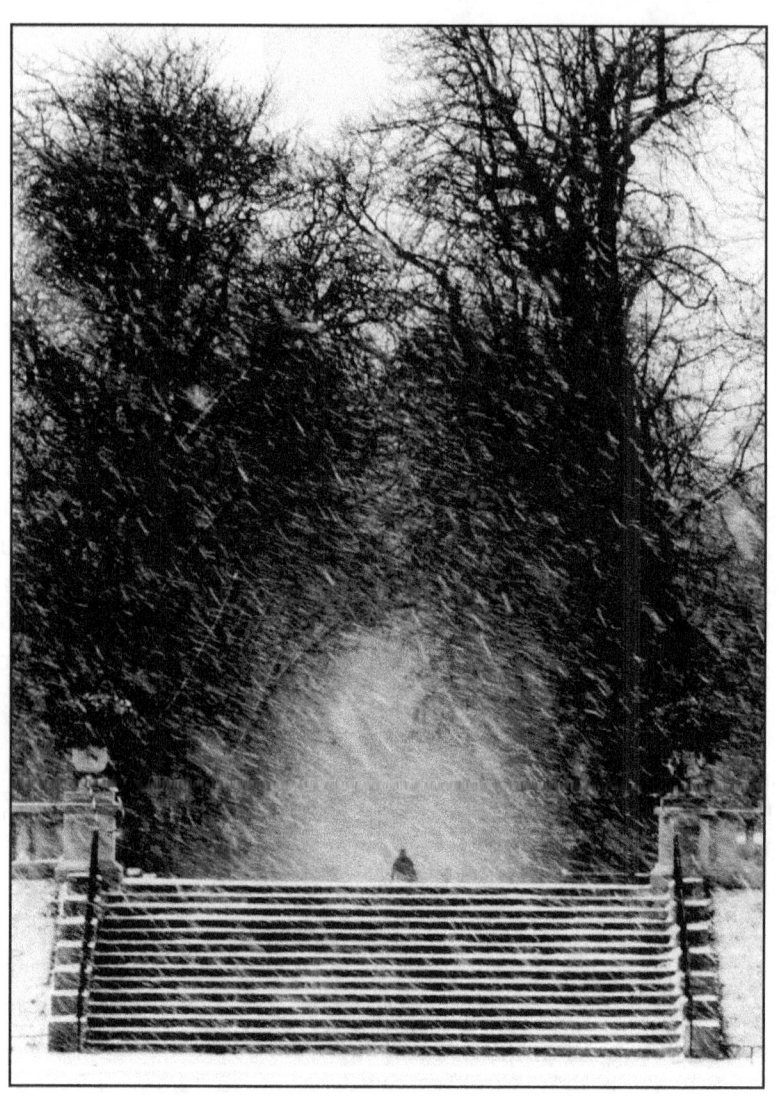

White Storm

"And there he was, another soul walking the gardens. I knew why I was there, but as I watched him walk away, I wondered; why was he?"

Paris, France

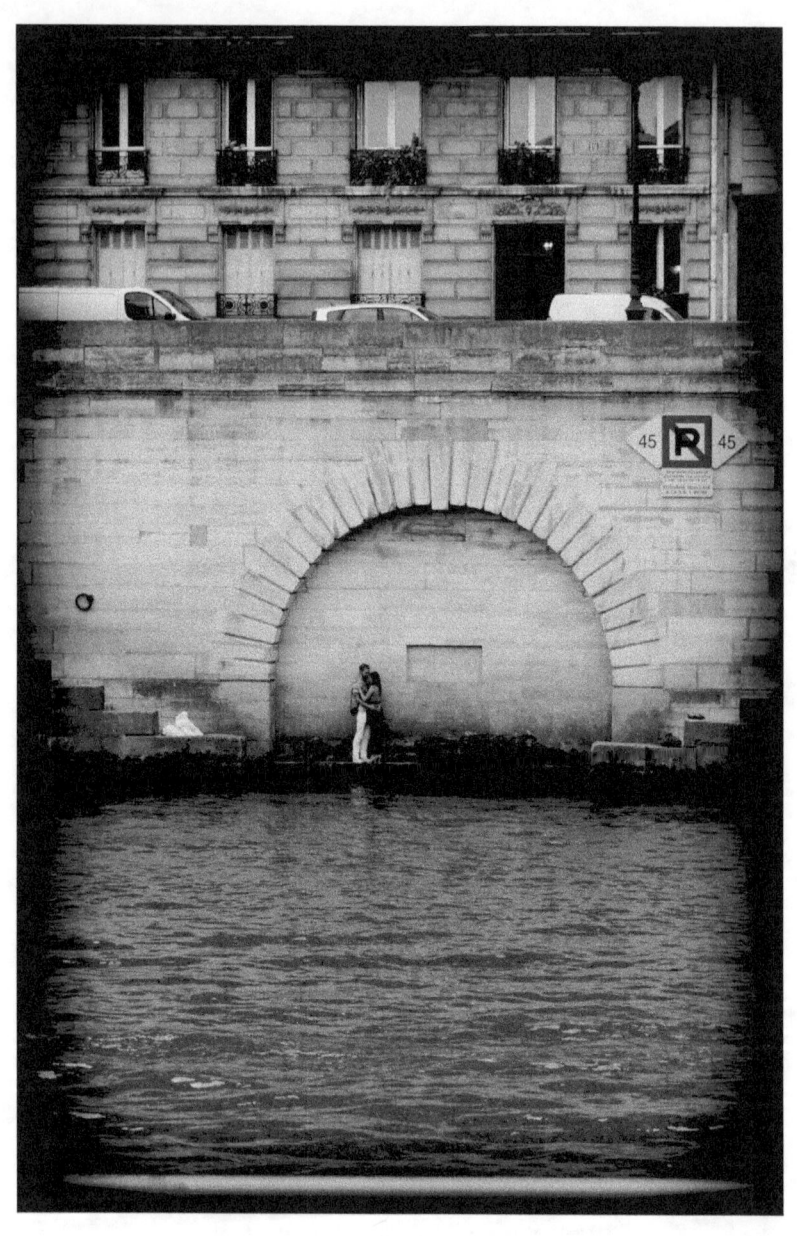

Quai de Seine

Paris, France

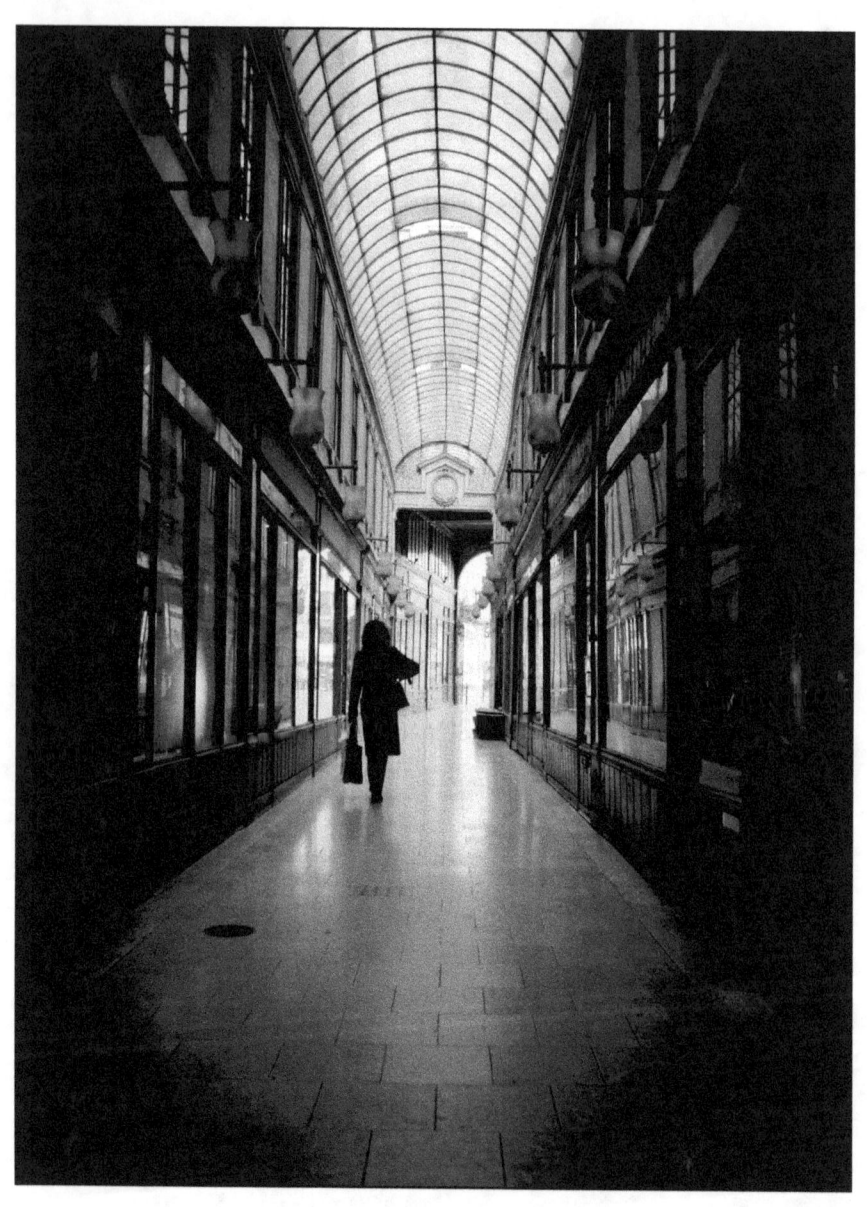

Passage du Bourg-L'Abbé

Paris, France

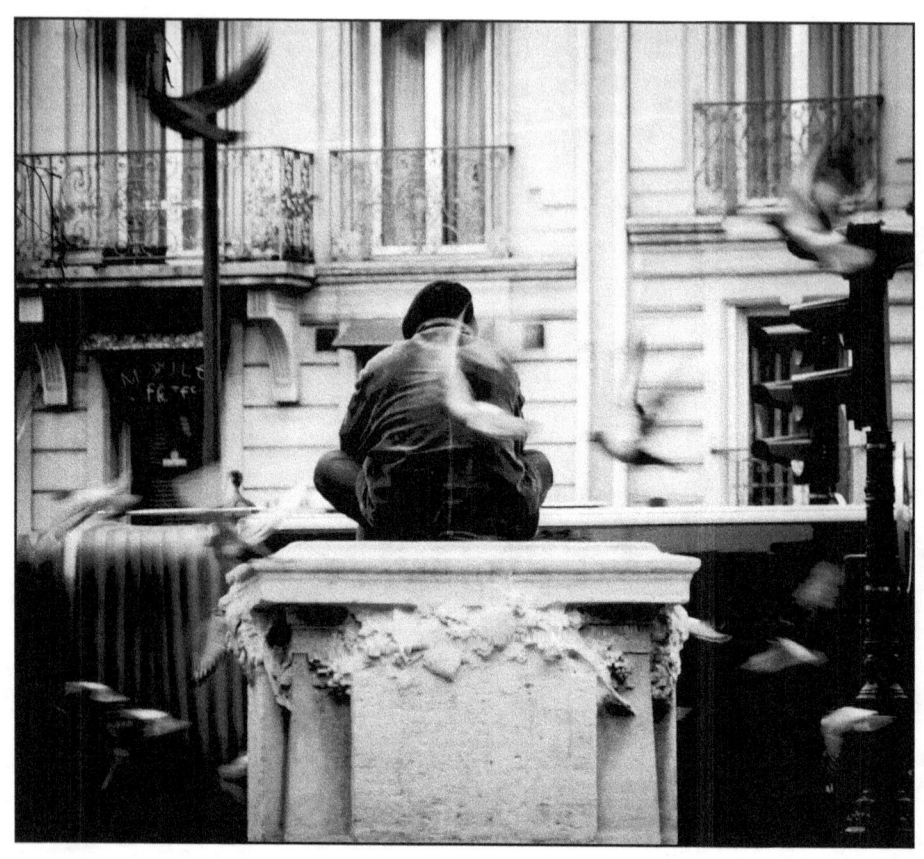

Statue

"I ran a cross this man sitting on top of a pedestal, where one would normally expect to find a statue. He was watching the day unfold before him, unnoticed by most and ignored by others. As the city harshly and uncaringly rushed by him, the way cities tend to, I smiled at the idea of man imitating art instead of art trying to imitate man."

Paris, France

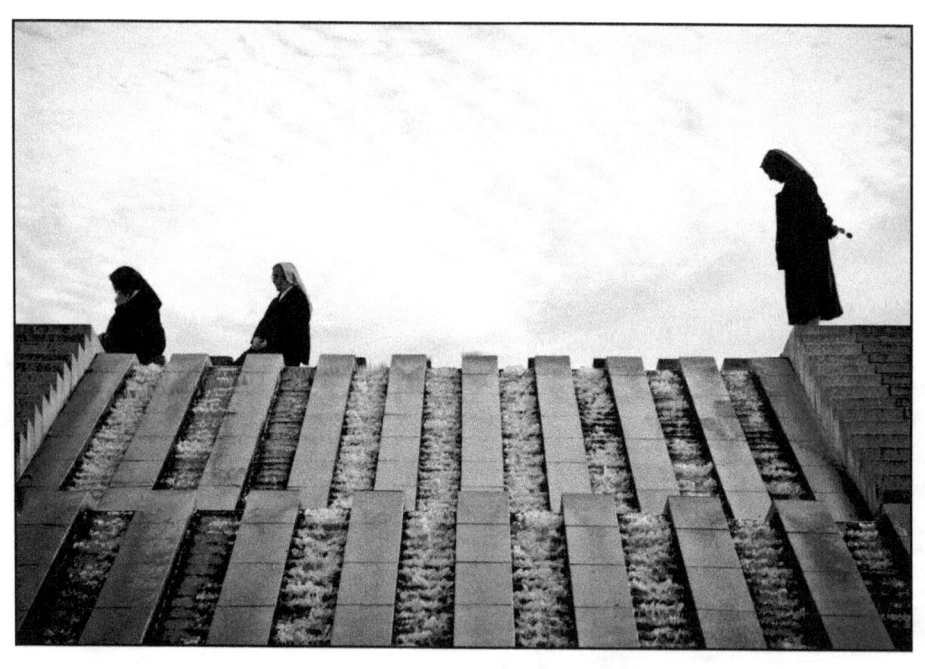

Heavens and Nuns

Paris, France

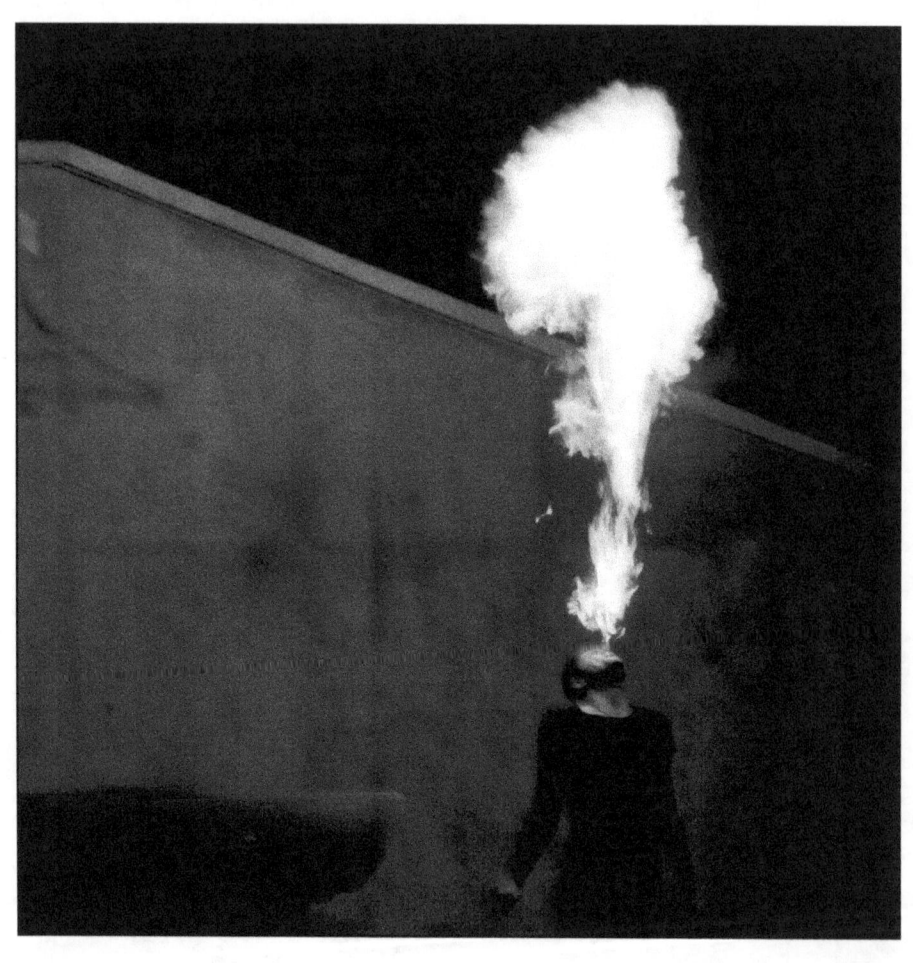

Spirit

Paris, France

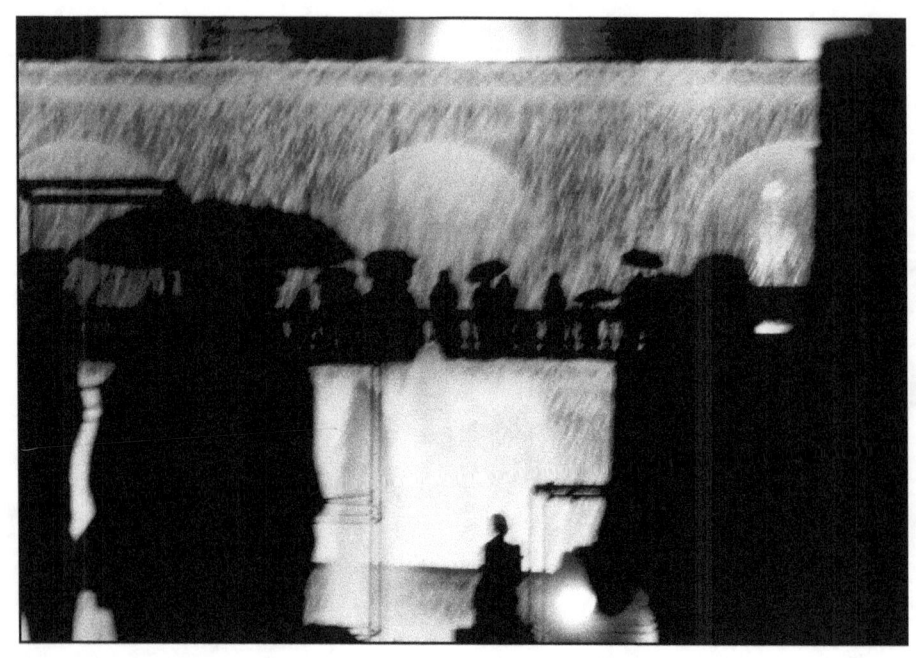

Barcelona Rain

Barcelona, Spain